MILKING THE BEAST WITHIN
SELECTED POEMS

MILKING THE BEAST WITHIN

The Selected Poems
Of

BEN DOUGLASS

Edited by
Rowena White

ATOMIC MOUNTAIN PRESS, LLC
Kashi Hara, Nara Ken, Japan
Toronto, Ontario, Canada
Hartford, Connecticut, USA
Portland, Oregon, USA

ATOMIC MOUNTAIN PRESS, LLC

Portions of this work originally appeared in "Small Voices, Big Words" Literary Review between 1978-1981.

BEN DOUGLASS: Milking the Beast Within. Copyright © 2021 by Ronald Dwayne Douglass.

Library of Congress Control Number: 2022902137

ISBN: 978-0-578-97972-4 (Paperback Edition)

SAN: 992-3705

COVER: Albert Birkle, The Acrobat, 1921, Weimer Republic

Established 2021
Oregon Office of:

**Atomic Mountain Press, LLC
5325 N.E. 37th Avenue
Portland, Oregon. 97211
USA
Cell Phone: 503-956-0500
Email:** atomicmountainpress@protonmail.com

Advanced Praise for **Milking the Beast Within**

Milking the Beast Within is the story of one man's life told in narrative poems. His poetry at times, are emotionally raw and biting, not unlike some of the Beat poets of the 50's and 60's. One can certainly see his growth and maturity as a poet and human being from youth to old age.

Alain Fabreau
Arles, France

This slim volume of poesy is a fast read. Even so, I found myself going back and pondering on certain poems and trying to figure out what really motivated the author: finding answers to life's hardest questions or just living life to the fullest and recording it. An excellent read that will earn space on one's bookshelf. Can't wait for the published copy to arrive.

Hans Angert
Meissen, Saxony, Germany

The poems included in this little book speak volumes about the inner life of the author. He pulls no punches from possibly offending polite society. This is evident, especially in his remarkable poem, "Saturday Night Poetry Reading with Beatrice." It caused me a hard blush. But it was a well-constructed poem about intimacy. I look forward to the published edition.

Linda Gales-Merck
Squamish, B.C., Canada

You won't want to miss this small book of poems by an Indie author from Portland, Oregon. His poetic stanzas come from the heart and soul. You can see an evolutionary pattern from start to finish. In his youth he was captivated with the religious side of life and then finally settled into an acceptance of what life IS and not what he wanted it to BE. Bravo, Mr. Douglass!

Danny Harris
Hartford, Connecticut, USA

A nice volume of poetry from a relatively unknown author who hails from the Pacific Northwest. His poems are essentially windows on how he viewed the world and himself at several stages of his life. I look forward to more of the same.

Susan Braun
Astoria, Oregon, USA

DEDICATION

FOR

AVE MARIE HANLON

Who has nourished my soul with courage, strength and happiness
over these many years.

Toward a characterization of modernity – overabundant
development of intermediary forms; atrophy of types; traditions
break off, schools; the overlordship of the instincts (prepared
philosophically: the unconscious worth more) after the will to power,
the willing of the ends and means, has been weakened.

Friedrich Nietzsche
From: The Will to Power

The unconscious is that chapter of my history which is marked by a
blank or occupied by a falsehood: it is the censored chapter.

Jacques Lacan
From: The Language of the Self

I have to speak, whatever that means. Having nothing to say, no
words but the words of others, I have to speak. No one compels me
to, there is no one, it's an accident, a fact. Nothing can ever exempt
me from it, there is nothing, nothing to discover, nothing to recover,
nothing that can lessen what remains to say.

Samuel Beckett
From: The Unnamable

AUTHOR PREFACE

This slim volume is a selection of my poems over the years. I decided to gather them in chronological order so the reader can see a pattern of growth over the years. The poems were chosen because they were written during times of difficult transitions.

As for the title of this volume, *Milking the Beast Within*: We all have a beast within us. A beast filled with all the human passions, waiting to come out and play. Most tie up that beast or drug it or beat it down and lock it away in a dark closest. Some let the beast out to do its bidding like, Cavafy, Pound, Jeffers, Cummings, Purdy, Bukowski, Sexton, Rukeyser, and Szymborska. Not only did they let the beast out to roam the public streets without a leash but milked that beast for everything it was worth.

This little **Chapbook** is my beast, my madness, my passion.

Ben Douglass
August 30, 2021

FORWARD

Mr. Douglass' *Milking the Beast Within* is an incredible romp of deeply personal prose poetry over a nearly fifty-year period. Some of these poems were originally published in my literary magazine, "Small Voices, Big Words" during the late nineteen seventies. Douglass sent me one hundred twenty poems for this **Chapbook**, and I settled on the ones presented here after careful selection and editing.

One can easily see the evolution of his poetry which followed his own life path: from youthful exuberance searching for the meaning of life, to the gritty reality in his middle age, to his philosophical acceptance in his senior years. This selection of poems tells the story of a Postmodern American man in search of self in a confusing, chaotic world.

If you enjoy the poems of Arthur Rimbaud and the prose of Jean Genet, you will certainly find a home in Douglass' poetry. Like his literary mentors before him, Jeffers, Pound, Szymborska, Mr. Douglass can be classified in the literary subgenres of **dirty realism** and **transgressive fiction**.

Rowena White
January 12, 2022

死
生活
DEATH LIFE

SITTING

March 1971

Sitting in grass
Disturbing it not
Listening
To the sermons of
Blue Jays & crickets

THE DRIFTER

July 1972

The drifter travels an empty highway
Frantically seeking his next birthday.
Finding not the answer but another dream
He stumbles forward through history with a scream.
Where will he find his mystical fate?
Does he know the hour is late?
When will he finally face his doom?
When will the wildflowers not bloom?
Why does he choose this lonely path?
Does he know it may incur God's wrath?
Who is this being with his own story?
Could he simply be a footnote in history?

The drifter walks to a frantic inward beat…
And the Mystic Drum never skips a beat!

MY RELIGION

Winter 1973

I have found my own private religion,
A religion that has yet to be named
And hopefully never will.
It is an authentic religion.
Its creed my own beating heart.
Its dogma my aging bones.
Its vision the synapses of my brain.
Its tradition: my birth, childhood,
Adolescence, adulthood.
It is a living, breathing, vibrant religion.
I am its deity, savior, chief disciple,
Follower and critic all rolled in one.
It is an exclusive religion.
It is MY religion.

EIGHTEEN MONTHS

January 1974

My mother tells me:

"As I held you at eighteen months,
While standing at our kitchen window,
I looked out and was amazed at what I saw,
Silver Creek over running its banks.
As a roof of a small house floated before me,
I got frightened and then you cried out.
This was the year we had to evacuate
Our little home.
The Red Cross gave us blankets, food & shelter."

TULOCAY CEMETARY

February 1974

As a child (age 5)?
Driving with father to the pig farm,
We would pass this strange, foreboding place.
Twice we stopped to pay homage to
Relatives who resided there for eternity.
The above ground crypts seemed like fairy castles
With strange words on them.
Twisted and deformed tombstones were
Dirty white with greenish mold bursting from the cracks.
From the southern direction
Take highway 29,
Turn right at Imola Avenue.
At the fifth stoplight,
Turn left onto Soscal Avenue.
At third stoplight
Bear right onto Silverado Trail.
Turn right onto Coombsville Road.
It is on the left.
As a young man (age19)?
Driving with parents to Tulocay
To send off my great aunt Vera.
The family crypt still
Strange and foreboding as ever.

HAPPINESS

February 1974

It was the summer of nineteen-sixty
In Napa, California
And I was five years old.
Gas was thirty cents a gallon,
First class stamps a mere four cents,
Popular radio song "Cathy's Clown"
By the Everly Brothers,
Put the worm in my young ear.
Harper Lee just released
To Kill a Mockingbird,
The adult world all-abuzz over
Russia shooting down Francis Gary Powers'
U-2 spy plane.
I remember this summer,
One of the happiest of my childhood.

FORBES MANSION

March 1976

The Forbes Mansion.
That's what we called it.
A three-story dumpy Victorian conversion
On third avenue, across from Napa City Bakery.
Two furnished one-bedroom apartments on first floor.
Single rooms on the second & third floors:
Shared bathroom and shower.
Owned by one John Forbes – Slumlord par excellence.
I rented the first one-bedroom apartment on the ground floor.
(Five-hundred fucking dollars a month)
Big picture window framed by stained-glass,
Leaded lattice work, facing the bakery storefront.
Beautiful but faded architecture inside & out.
Residents mostly unemployed, on food stamps,
Using and dealing dope: reds, coke, pot, whatever.
Beating their girlfriends into quiet submission weekly,
While playing loud rock music or television.
(Walls paper thin)
Friday nights when I couldn't write or read,
When radio reception was clear, I would listen to
The "Adventures of Cinnamon Bear"
(From Portland, Oregon)
While drinking Old English 800 forty ouncers.
I could then finally sleep, despite the shattering
Activity throughout the house.

HARD LABOR

June 1976

The work was exceedingly hard, dead exhausting.
I was not use to such hard work.
My fanciful mind would make many journeys to the
Kingdom of Tibet,
Having discussions with Swami's of a High Order.
Sometimes (on difficult days) I pictured myself in a
Concentration Camp, pulling bodily remains
From still hot ovens, shouting, weeping,
Near collapse!
The forklift driver would take me down to reality,
Dumping another pallet next to me.
I would open the little door to the fifteen-foot circular
Wooden drum, water, solutions, pouring out onto me.
Pulling wet sheepskin hides onto the pallet,
In a locking formation to reach six-foot high,
Would take me thirty-minutes to get ten hides on a pallet.
PATHETIC! EMBARRASING!
(I once wet my shorts)
Others down the line of drums would stare, make faces,
Then brutally laugh, pointing at the weak, fragile,
Mr. Know-it-All, who read books on his lunch break.
Unlike the boys down the line, I didn't eat reds like candy.
Just dreamed, then waited for ten-minute breaks & lunch.
At night my arms were so heavy I could not type or even
Pick up a book to read.
They finally moved me elsewhere.
(There is a god)!

CANTICA AFFLICTUS HOMO AMERICANUS

August 1976

The song of an afflicted American man,
Hard to hear and worse to see.
He believes the world hasn't changed (much)
Since that Great Conflagration that was WW2.
Unbeknownst to him a separate Reality has arrived,
It came like a thief in the night – during –
Alcohol, drugged sleep.
He continues to walk the streets of
Darkened, troubled cities that are just as clueless
As our afflicted American man,
Shaking his fist at passerby, he shouts:
"What have you done to my Reality, my Dream, my Life?"
"......................."
He walks slowly & deliberately into the countryside
Still not aware what really happened or how
He sits under a big green tree under a big blue sky
And puts a bullet in his brain.

DO NOT BE LIKE THEM

January 1977

Read Pound, Joyce, Elliot, Cummings, Cavafy, Jeffers,
Kaufman, Ginsburg, LeRoi Jones (Amiri Baraka)!
Cogitate upon their words, their wisdom or not wisdom.
Understand how they changed themselves and (the World),

But do not be like THEM,
And do not write like THEM.
   (.....it cannot be done, baby,
   even if attempted,
   will turn out BAD, very BAAAAAAAAAAAA.....).

Live your own motherfuckin' miserable life,
Create your own style: *Pretense. Attitude. Myth. Life.*

   (.....be like rancid, broken cream in a jar,
   not like fluffy white from a can.
   force them to drink. Deeply drink.
   then you have them, they are yours forever.
   others will follow just to taste your shit,
   because they know you are YOU
   and not like THEM.....).

A SOLITARY FIGURE

January 1977

A solitary figure,
Standing motionless (in wind, rain)
On Market Street (in San Francisco).
Cars, buses, trolleys, busy people, lonely people,
Drunks, whores, pimps, drug dealers,
Gawking tourists, coppers on their beat,
Go on by with attention riveted forward, elsewhere.
A solitary figure,
Holds a stack of newspapers wrapped in plastic,
Headline: "Socialist Workers Condemn Reagan!"
With sunken hungry eyes, beseeching, begging, and hoping,
A solitary figure,
Holds out a paper for only a dollar but,
Nobody is buying today, or yesterday, or before that.
A solitary figure,
Standing motionless (in wind, rain)
On Market Street (in San Francisco).

ON READING BUKOWSKI FOR THE FIRST TIME

January 1977

I felt the need to take a long, hot shower, with lots of soap,
And then repeat it again and again.
A drunken, lowlife asshole from the L.A. Underground,
Who treats women, fellow writers & fans equally shitty,
But who loves animals, especially cats!
The *BUK'S* (rhymes with PUKE?) writing style
Workman-like, simple, direct, unpretentious.
Much like Hemingway, he admits.
He uses his stories & poems to depict
The depravity of American culture, high and low.
He is a lowlife nihilist much like the Russian writers
During the Golden Age of the 19th century, but
I am unable to tear away my eyes from his words.
I come back for more, like a beaten child who continues
Coming back home to the abusive father,
Asking for yet another smack upside the head.

DAY

May 1977

I burst into the glorious sunlight
    from the dark shadows of my soul.

I had been gone so long
    lost among the shadows of my soul.

But this April morning has drawn me
    to its sunshine & warmth of my soul.

And I leave once more
    the night of that sheltered womb of my soul.

LOOKING INWARD AND OUTWARD

May 1977

Looking inward (contemplating) two hours daily,
Trying to separate soul from body
And traverse the God Worlds of Eckankar.

No luck after days, weeks, months.
Only strange, putrid, naughty dreams after eating a
Nine-day old tuna sandwich withering in the icebox.

Looking outward – the world:
Drinking, fucking, working, shitting, paying bills, reading,
Singing, playing, dreaming, hoping. REAL LIFE?

Looking inward: travelling deep valleys of emptiness and despair,
Thick tomes of magical thinking follow me,
That bring forth questionable visions. REAL LIFE?

What's left?
That Great Expanse of the
Vague, grey, murky middle where truth resides.

BEATRICE

July 1977

O, Dearest Beatrice, My Beatrice…..

When you came into my life and touched me
    To the core of my Being. A whispered
    Silent melody filled my heart.

The voice of stillness broke across the
Synapses of my brain, like the sea
    Crashing to the shore, deep and moving
    In harmony with an ancient, timeless score.

CAN LIFE BE ANYMORE THAN THIS?

August 1977

Saturday.
Sitting on the bank of the Napa River
(not too far from Sawyer Tanning Company).
Me and Beatrice
(my French Creole Queen)
And
A 4-liter jug of Dago Red.
Reading poems to each other from Paul Twitchell's
Stranger by the River.
Puffy white clouds like cotton candy on this warm,
Breezy noon. Sail boats off in the distance,
Slicing water like a hot knife through butter.

MY CONSORT

August 1977

My Consort,
(my French Creole Queen).
Her skin the color of roasted coffee beans
(decaf).
Lips moist, inviting, trembling. Beckoning.
No one like her
(not even in Ebony Magazine).
Her countenance sparkles like a
Thousand-million suns and moons.
(Like the Spiral Nebulae)!
When she smiles, night becomes day,
Day becomes like summer wine.
Why her? Why me? Gift of the gods?
Maybe just a fluke, maybe real, maybe nothing!
I will take it – whatever it is.

MOVING HISTORY

August 1977

She drove a faded orange Volkswagen bug:
Many dents and scraps, hole in floorboard,
Cracked rear window, license plate loosey-goosey.
  (you know what I'm talking about,
  the kind held together
  by its paint job)

Many miles, many passengers, many tears, many joys, many
Arguments, many parking tickets on the windshield.
A rolling adventure of revolutionary fervor:

Journeys to People's Park,
  City Lights Bookshop,
    Jack London Square,
      Concerts,
        Protests,
          Riots,
            Food pantries,
              The S.F. Aquarium,
                And much. Much more.

Long nights along North Beach, smoking weed,
Drinking Port wine, having sex in the back seat,
While hookers, johns, pimps, dealers, hipsters
Walk by trying not to notice the gentle rocking.

SATURDAY NIGHT POETRY READING

August 1978

Beatrice my French Creole Queen…..

Sat across from me,

Blue satin robe falling open,

Legs crossed, bare feet, painted pink toenails.

Skin like creamy brown café ole coffee.

Her left hand held a silver cigarette holder.

Puffing on a Benson and Hedges Virginia Red,

Wisps of blue smoke curled upward like

Dancing ghosts above her head.

Her right hand held a thin, ragged copy of

"Solitudes Crowded with Loneliness"

By beat poet Bob Kaufman.

Between drags on her cigarette she

Read aloud to me the amazing lines.

After fifteen minutes she finally stood,

Laying down cigarette and book,

Her blue satin robe revealing everything.

She came over, bent low, whispered in my ear,

Walked down the hallway with grace & beauty

Of an Egyptian goddess, dropping her blue satin robe,

Before entering the bedroom.

I sat there for a few minutes longer nursing

My flute of Korbel champagne and

Pondering the words of the great poet,

As spoken by my Beatrice.

I finally stood, disrobed, walked down the hallway.

Entering the bedroom, I was met with soft sounds of the

"Rivers of Babylon" by Boney M, coming from

Her 8-track player.

She lay across the bed covers, eyes glowing green,

Her supple body glistened with essential oil.

Her breast stood erect…quivering.

She stretched her arms above her head.

I stood poised: nude, hard, stiff, throbbing…

Yearning for what was to come.

I went down hard on her like a dog in heat.

She grabbed my face, sucking life out of my body,

Wrapping her legs around me vise-like,

Like a wild woman thirsting for water after a long draught,

Begging, moaning, sighing, digging fingernails into my back.

I, her, we, became one with the universe that evening.

Saturday night poetry readings would never be the same.

THE PASSING OF BEATRICE

January 1980

I remember the day well. It was a clear, crispy
Morning in late October, in Oakland, California.
The sun sat high in the blue sky like a
Great yellow frozen disc (unplugged, unconcerned)
Shadows everywhere seemed cold, oddly sinister.
I walked street after street for hours, numb,
An empty shell of a human being. Past
Intersections, parks, schools, storefronts, I walked,
Remembering delightful memories of my one true love.

-Beatrice?
-Why?
-What made you do this?
-It didn't have to end like this, there was an
-Escape hatch waiting for you to enter.

My Beatrice, who boldly stepped into the
Great Inky Expanse we call Eternity to
Parts unknown, never to return.

-Did you not once
-Think of those left behind?

[…gnashing their teeth…shaking…screaming…crying,
    …forlorn…derelict…angry…confused…wanting…]

-NO, YOU PROBABLY DID NOT!

CLARITY, OR HELLO KRISHNAMURTI

October 1980

1.

Like others before me,
Since the dawn of time,
I seek something.
Beyond myself.
  Beyond this Earth.
    Beyond the Universe.
      Beyond Spacetime itself.
I call it Truth, God, First Principle,
A timeless state of Eternity
Providence.

2.

I have always asked the BIG questions:
-What is it all about?
-Has life meaning?
All I see, however, day in, day out,
Personal brutality,
Social chaos,
Famine,
War,
Endless divisions of humanity by
Money, skin color, class, creed, age, sex.

3.

Finally, I settle on FAITH, faith in a Guru
But Guru's, like cheap wine, always disappoint…
Always…always…always…
And FAITH eventually breeds violence.

The cycle of existential despair goes…
On…and on…and on…and on…
I must jump off the merry-go-round of seeking,
But…fear…there's always fear…of the UNKNOWN.
4.

Maybe the UNKNOWN isn't so bad after all.
Maybe it's simply this:
-A shot of whisky,
-A beautiful woman,
-A new car,
-A new house…with kids,
-A good poem,
-A good book.
IS THAT ALL THERE IS?
Maybe I'm just deceiving myself
With the glitter and toys of mundane
Material Life.
REPLACEMENTS FOR ETERNAL LIFE?

5.

Maybe I should stop seeking both
And SEE…really SEE…
What happens in fragile moments
(WITH CLARITY OF MIRTH!!!)
Satori, split-second, keep going.

CREATION

October 1983

FIRST DAY: Big Bang
SECOND DAY: Great Expansion
THIRD DAY: universes, nebulae, galaxies, stars, planets, moons
Birthed into the emptiness of spacetime
FOURTH DAY: Primordial Soup bubbled, gurgled, snapped,
crackled, and popped on lucky orbiting rocks
FIFTH DAY: little Blue Dot in darkest corner of Milky Way
Waited patiently for its turn
(Eternity to the 10th power?)
SIXTH DAY: millions, billions, trillions of
Asteroids with magical frozen water showered the
BLUE DOT
And co-mingled with the Hot Soup
SEVENTH DAY: Life started on its gruesome and
Harrowing journey to
What It IS!

BECOMING 1

(When demons, monsters & brutes walked the Earth)

October 1983

5 million BCE: Australopithecus walks the open spaces of Africa
2 million BCE: Homo habilis develops tools for survival against hostile environs
1 million BCE: Homo erectus uses fire for better life, still not good
250,000 BCE: Early Homo sapiens use stone tools, live by hunting & gathering in the Paleolithic era
100,000 BCE: Homo sapiens migrate out of Africa
45,000 BCE: Settlement of Australia begins. Stone-tipped spears developed
40,000 BCE: Homo sapiens make cave paintings
30,000 BCE: Humans migrate from Asia to North America via land bridge across the Bering Strait
25,000 BCE: Use of ceramics for food & water storage begins to develop
20,000 BCE: Bows & arrows are first used
11,000 BCE: Land bridge across Bering Strait covered by water during receding Ice Age

BECOMING 2

(When witch doctors, sorcerers & holy men ruled)

October 1983

Oracles of all creeds, colors and shapes
Binding men, women, children into slavery
With their castle's-in-the-sky sermons, platitudes,
Tricks and magic.
Then came the
ENLIGHTENMENT, then
JAZZ, then
HUMANISM, then
Chipping away at the Golden Chains
Still chipping, chipping, chipping, however.
Ah.....history!

ALONE

November 1984

A Sunday alone,
Upstairs, La Patisserie,
4th & N.E. Everett, PDX.
Café crowded, people waiting, people smoking
Clove cigarettes.
Sipping Mexican mocha,
Eating strawberry scone
Thinking of future tense:
Poverty & obscurity & meaninglessness.
A controlled death on credit.

WOULD IT NOT BE FUN?

November 1984

Would it not be fun
Drinking strong black coffee,
In a café on a rainy November in
PDX, observing a conversation
Between George Orwell & Ayn Rand?

DEVILS & SAINTS

November 1984

While sitting with John
(on a cold November morning)
Sharing a large pot of
Russian Caravan tea at
La Patisserie,
We overheard Ernie (another morning regular)
Booming voice, shaking finger at half sleep girl
Two tables away:
"The devil and the saint are cut from the same cloth."
John looked at me with his coal black eyes:
"It's all about nuance, complexity and
Power over people."
He raised his tea mug high and
Snickered at the obscurity of it all.

NUANCE

November 1984

The Marxist claims Truth
The Anarcho-Libertarian claims Truth
They can't both be right (or wrong!)
They can't see the Great Muddy Middle
Where Truth hides like a scared rabbit
Deep in a long dark cave
So says my other friend, Ernie
For he's been on both sides
And now clumsily walks the fence top

IN PRAISE OF CAVAFY

December 1984

This great Greek poet
Now celebrated throughout
The Western world.
His greatness has steadily
Grown since World War One
The consummate master at
Scene presentation, intense feeling,
And direct, unornamented verse.
His poetry is erotic
And openly homosexual.
His principle themes are
Love, art and politics
Finely tuned by his Greek sense.
Born of Greek parents in
Alexandria, Egypt, where
He lived and died:
The greatest modern Greek poet.

THE MASTER WORK

December 1984

A sixty-year-old book
Heavy, dense tome
(500,000 words)
Of yellowed pages
Exuding a perfume of
Yesterday's wisdom
That speaks of humanity
(man's tears and all that)
Past, present and future
It's author now exhausted
Broken, recycled
Lost in time to generations
Forgotten among today's
Young and brave of heart
Who read and write bumper stickers
A sad tale of our times

REMEMBERING JEFFERS

January 1985

I find it impossible to imagine how anyone
Can read the lilting, lyrical poems
Of Robinson Jeffers, and not perceive greatness.
His narrative poems rival Wordsworth.
Electrifying, making goosebumps.
The world will lose something of deep value
If ever we let his words slip away.
With words he paints a stunning picture of
California's peculiar ambiance
With unsurpassed vividness.
He lived, breathed and felt the sublime
Shoreline of California's north coast, with a
Lyrical meditative passion so complete.

ABSOLUTE ZEN

August 1989

To my right,
    Piles of books;

To my left,
    A coffee mug;

In front of me,
    A wall filled with 3X5 note cards;

Behind me,
    My cat Verne licking his ass;

There is no greater happiness than this.
    Here, Now!

ABSOLUTE ZEN…...

THE BEAST WITHIN

June 1990

We all have a beast within,
Not the vampiric, blood-sucking,
Monstrosity you see at the
Neighborhood theater.
No.

The beast within is much like you and me.
This beast is much more sophisticated.
It goes by different names and takes on
Different forms as needed:
The angry, drunken father who
Beats you without rhyme or reason;
The emotionally distant mother who
Refused to intervene;
The bottle of Scotch so you could forget the
Sins of the Father and Mother;
The abusive mate who sucks you dry of
Feeling, money, everything;
The employer who treats you like
A slave and tricks you at every turn.

Let the beast rule & play havoc on your life
If you will, until the day they plant you
Under the ground.

Or,
Tame the beast, direct its energy to
Something Higher.
Use the beast for your creation.
Take it off the leash
Let it run wild for a season
Or two

Before locking it away again in the
Closet whence it lived.

SITTING AT THE TYPER

July 1993

When I type a line, a page, a thesis
I do not represent the communities of
Baby Boomers, White Anglo-Saxon Protestants,
Hipsters, Vegans, New Agers, Buddhists, or Atheists.

I put words to paper to discover the guts of
My heart, mind & soul. This process I call
The Wonderful Country. It gives me
The wherewithal to survive this viral
Infection called Humanity.

When I do poetry, I am
Building a moat around the Castle of my Fragile Self
Filled with snakes, crocs and other nasties.
My readers (or admirers) are allowed to
Peer at me across the moat but will
Never access the Castle of my Fragile Self.
That will always be off limits.

THE OLD POET

February 1999

This old poet dreams forgotten
Words once alive and green
That brought pretty, young girls with
Dresses and sashes of Spring & Summer
Squealing and clapping with
Magnificent ecstasy.

Somewhere far and away in
A corner of a faded, dusty room
In a blighted, cold, forsaken house
Deep in a neglected, gnarly
Forest of dead brambles, thorns and
Forgotten vineyards;
This old poet dreams.

LET IT BE

August 2010

Through highs & lows of perpetual destruction
Of marital bliss, the sun sets one last time,
Finally.....forever and not to
Death do us part.

Breaking the surface, gulping oxygen, looking
At a world I haven't seen in many years.
It's a familiar, peaceful, sobering sight
To behold. Unlike the drunken shadow that
Stalked my days.

As I open the door to a new day and trip
Over empty bottles of Rum, Rye and Vodka,
I pause long enough and look back at the
Shadow reclining on the couch.

Who will take care of the little furry ones,
The creatures who depend on us for everything.
I mumble and cry in sadness and confusion.
The fickle hand of Fate grabs my hand and says:
"Run. Run like you've never run before."

[The air is alive with strains of the Beatles song,
"Let It BE." I start running, running
As fast as the wind pushes my back
Towards a new day, a new path, a new journey.]

THE MYSTERY OF MAN AND WOMAN

September 2012

A darkened stage. Small red light blinking in background,
Like morse code. Subdued yellowish light clicks on,
Illuminating stage, mostly barren, empty. Completely dreary.
Two small ratty wooden chairs sit center stage. Between them
A large bowl of rotting fruit, on a small red circular stand.
A white table stage left has a cell phone on it.
Black curtains drape the back wall and sides.

SCENE 1

A naked woman enters stage left,
Sits in chair on the left. Stares intently
At the audience.
A naked man enters stage right,
Sits in chair on the right. Stares intently
At the audience.
Both keep staring for ten minutes,
Without expression on their faces.
The audience starts fidgeting, looking at each other.
Murmurs start moving throughout the theater.
The lights go out, everything in darkness,
Except for the small red blinking light.
This goes on for one minute. More murmurs,
Growing across the audience.

SCENE 2

Bright white lights flash on, illuminating
The stage,
Bleeding down into the audience. The

Nude couple are still there, expressionless.
The woman sharply turns her head,
Looking at the man.
"I don't want you anymore. I don't need you."
The man slowly turns his head,
Looking at the woman.
"Why?"
"Just because," says she, as she grimaces
At the audience.
The woman quickly jumps up, walking to the table,
Picking up the cell phone. She frantically starts
Swiping and punching the screen.
A look of contentment grows across her face
As she lay the cell phone down, and runs off
Stage left.
The man ever so slowly rises from the chair,
Lumbering towards the table. He picks up the cell phone
And slowly swipes and punches the screen.
Suddenly a look of horror crawls across his face
As he lay the cell phone down, and slowly ambles
Across to stage right and exits.
The stage again is plunged into darkness. Murmurs
And rustling can be heard from the audience.

SCENE 3

A loud CRACK of a whip.
Suddenly multicolored lights bath the stage and audience.
Calliope music permeates the theater.
A man dressed like a circus ringmaster stands
Behind the two chairs, a hand resting on each.
Shouting at the top of his voice the man proclaims,
"I wish I could offer some advice or meaning or
Hope about what you have seen. I can't.
But this I can offer to the audience tonight."
He then walks over to the white table, picks up
The cell phone and drops it on the floor. He then
Stomps hard on it several times until it is
Completely shattered. He turns briefly to

The audience and pauses briefly, then
Walks off stage left.
Darkness falls on the theater. All that can be seen is
The small blinking red light at the back of the stage.
Someone in the audience lights up his face with
A flashlight and screams loudly,
"Is this all there is?"

finis

**The Author
Ben Douglass
Spring 2018**

ABOUT THE AUTHOR

For the last 40-years, the author has lived in Portland, Oregon. The last 34 of those years he has lived in the Concordia neighborhood of Northeast Portland, with his beloved partner, Ave Marie, and two dogs and five cats.

Ben Douglass was born and raised in Napa, California until age 6, when the family moved to Hayward, California, where he graduated from Hayward High School in 1974.

He has held the following jobs in his long-varied working life: Church janitor, burger flipper, tannery worker, leather coat factory cutter, mechanics helper at a garment factory, high-rise security officer, suicide hotline worker, street youth outreach worker, transitional housing coordinator, assessment counselor at a methadone maintenance clinic, and finally, a 20-plus year run as a grocery worker and manager. The author is now retired.

The author has never stopped his continuing academic education, for he believes a culturally made person must keep learning until the day we die. He holds certificates in technical writing, creative writing, poetry, and an undergraduate certificate in systemic family therapy.

The author also has self-published numerous works under the name of Mercury Flats Publishing. Those works include a novella, short stories, essays, and a poetry collection called, *Beneath the Surface*.

ABOUT THE EDITOR

Rowena White is an 81-year-old woman who hails from Whitehall, New York. She graduated from Roosevelt High School with a standard diploma; graduated from City College of New York with a B.A in Classical Studies; graduated Cal-State Irvine with a M.A. in Japanese Language and Literature. She was founder and editor of Small Voices, Big Words Literary Review, which is now defunct. She went on to found and edit several such magazines during her lifetime, as well as a teacher of English in Japanese schools. Currently she is founder and Executive Editor of Atomic Mountain Press based in Kashi Hara, Japan.

ABOUT ATOMIC MOUNTAIN PRESS

Dedicated to reprinting forgotten works by various misfits, outsiders, and rebels. Also, to highlight the works of new independent authors who want nothing to do with the big corporate publishers. The underlying concept here is based on a few simple propositions:

A) That to be a success under the current definition is highly toxic – wealth, fame and power are a poison cocktail;

B) That this era of triumphal capitalism glorifies the dreariest human traits like greed and self-interest as good and natural;

C) That the "winners" version of reality and history is deeply lame and soul-rotting stuff.

Given this, it follows that the truly interesting and meaningful lives and real adventures are only to be had on the margins of what Kenneth Rexroth called "the social lie." It's with the dropouts, misfits, dissidents, renegades and revolutionaries, against the grain, between the cracks and amongst the enemies of the state that the good stuff can be found.

Fortunately, there is a mighty subterranean river of testimony from the disaffected, a large cache of hidden history, of public secrets overlooked by the drab conventional wisdom the **Atomic Mountain Press** aims to tap into. A little something to set against the crushed hopes, mountains of corpses, and commodification of everything. We think, it's the best thing Western Civilization has going for itself.

TIMES NEW ROMAN
(FONT HISTORY)

This project used the following font throughout its preparation.

Times New Roman gets its name from the Times of London, the British Newspaper. In 1929, the *Times* hired typographer Stanley Morison to create a new text font. Because it was used in a daily newspaper, the new font quickly became popular among printers of the day. The differences between its predecessor, Times Roman. The new font has thinner serifs, blunted terminals, and a rounded ear on the "g," as well as other more subtle refinements. The differences are noticeable when the fonts are enlarged side-by-side.

Reader Notes